What's Your Story?
Questions that Lead to Authentic,
Powerful Writing

Rachel Renee Smith

Rain Publishing

KNIGHTDALE, NORTH CAROLINA

Copyright © 2014 by **Rachel Renee Smith**

All rights reserved. No part of this publication may be reproduced, distributed or transmitted in any form or by any means, including photocopying, recording, or other electronic or mechanical methods, without the prior written permission of the publisher, except in the case of brief quotations embodied in critical reviews and certain other noncommercial uses permitted by copyright law. For permission requests, write to the publisher, addressed "Attention: Permissions Coordinator," at the address below.

Rachel Renee Smith/Rain Publishing, LLC
PO Box 702
Knightdale, NC 27545
www.rainpublishing.com

Cover design: Trevis C. Bailey, www.SDCreativeWorks.com

Edited by: Rain Publishing, LLC

Ordering Information: Quantity sales. Special discounts are available on quantity purchases by corporations, associations, and others. For details, contact the "Special Sales Department" at the address above.

What's Your Story?/ Rachel Renee Smith. – 1st ed.
ISBN 978-0-9908453-0-0

Library of Congress Catalog Number: 2014951730

This book is dedicated to everyone who has a story to share and the courage to tell it, especially the authors I have the pleasure of knowing.

Special thanks to God, who is my life, and my husband, Jeffrey LaMont Smith, who is my partner in everything.

Thank you to my amazing family Andrew Joseph, Nicole Griggs and Kendall Daniels, Barbara Griggs and Michael Nelson, Ronald Griggs and Vickie Holmes, Avie and Jamie Holmes, and to my valued extended family and friends.

Thank you to Linda Dominique and Calvin Holland for being the catalysts of my personal and professional growth.

Thank you Danielle and Hasani Pettiford for so generously sharing your knowledge and support through the years.

Thank you Paul Stankus for sharing those things that save authors a lot of grief!

Thank you Tina Bailey for catching the vision and running with it and for all of your support.

Thank you to all of our divine partners:

*Trevis and Ebony Bailey of
Sarah Denise Creative Works*

Author and Recording Artist Marcel Anderson

W.E. Da Cruz Communications

Author and Editor Sherrian Crumbley

The Grow Your Dreams Network

CONTENTS

Why am I Writing?..1
   How do I clarify purpose?...............................3
   Questions to Consider:......................................6
Who am I Writing To?..7
   What is it that they need?...............................10
   Why would they want to read my book?..........13
   How do I determine what questions my readers have?..14
   Questions to Consider:....................................23
How do I Keep Track of all This?.......................25
   Questions to Consider 31
What Do I Want them to Know?..........................33
   Where is the material coming from?...............35
   Questions to Consider 37
Is it Real Yet?..39
   Authenticity..41
   Brokenness...42
   Compassion..43
   Questions to Consider 45

Did I Wrap it in Love? 47
   Editing 48
   Graphic Design and Formatting: 49
Leaving it All on the Page 53
   Anything is Possible 54
Interview with Author Marcel Anderson 57
Testimonials 64

Introduction

Some of the most unforgettable moments of life are the ones where our burning questions have been answered. In fact, much of the anxiety that people experience is due to questions that have been left unanswered for long periods of time.

Look at this list and allow yourself to feel the emotions associated with these questions:

Does he/she love me?
Does anybody love me?
Am I lovable?
What is wrong with me?
Did I pass the test?
Will I be able to pay my bills?
How can I lose this weight?
Who are my real parents?
Will I ever get justice in my situation?
Will my circumstances change?
Will this person ever leave me alone?
How can I stop dating the wrong kinds of people?
Where can I find true love?
How can I start a business?

How do I write a book?
What do I need to know about marriage?
How can I deal with the death of my loved one?
How can I heal from abuse?

As a writing coach, I employ the use of questions all the time to not only help me understand what my writers' goals are, but also to help the writers clarify their goals, purpose, intentions, and major writing points. As we progress further into the writing process, I put myself in the seat of the reader and ask the questions that I believe they would be asking.

As you can imagine, going through this process of question and answer not only yields more detailed and interesting writing, it makes the story or message come alive and sometimes causes the author to deal with thoughts and emotions that they may not have delved into as deeply before. With the intention of writing to help and liberate someone else, the author frees themselves in the process.

Addressing your readers' questions gives you the opportunity to connect with them on a deeply intimate level without ever having a face-to-face conversation. Your reader will feel as if you intimately understand them when they turn the pages of your book and find the answers they have been seeking.

Throughout this book, I will ask many questions to help you exercise your mind and get to the information, and ultimately the words that you need for your book. As you read and consider the questions, please have a notebook and pen handy to help you begin to outline and map out your writing. The questions to help guide your writing are indexed in the table of contents should you ever want to refer back to them directly. Towards the end of this book, I have also included an interview with a bestselling author who shares how this method of coaching enhanced his writing process. If you have any questions along the way, feel free to email me at info@rachelreneesmith.com.

CHAPTER ONE

Why am I Writing?

You woke up, showered, brushed your teeth, combed your hair, and put on your finest outfit. Next, you made sure you had your phone, keys, sweater or jacket, and every essential on the checklist before walking out the front door and locking it. Then, you stood there for the rest of the day because you never really decided where you were going. Does that make any sense? Does that remotely seem like something you would actually do?

For most things that we put effort into, there is a purpose, even if that purpose does not immediately jump out at you. If you went through that routine and had nowhere to go, you may have done so in order to mentally prepare yourself for the tasks you had to complete that day, minus of course the part where you went outside and just stood in front of your door because you had nowhere to go. (I am not knocking you if you get all dressed up and stand in front of your door with nowhere to go! Do you really do that?)

Like waking up in the morning and preparing for your day, it would greatly serve you to have a purpose in mind when it comes to writing. You may desire to entertain, educate, inspire, minister, provoke, persuade, or all of the above with your writing. Your purpose and intention is up to you, but it is important that you become clear on your purpose.

There will be times when you are challenged in your writing process. The challenge may come in the form of what feels like writer's block, discouragement, negative feelings about whether your project will be received, or feeling lost and without direction, wondering what you are doing and feeling like you don't know the first thing about what you are doing. This is all normal. However, when you are clear on your "Why" it will help drive you through those difficult, challenging places in your creative process.

Being clear on the "Why" will also help you stay focused in your writing by organizing your thoughts and helping you quickly steer away from ideas that will confuse your reader because they don't quite fit in with the purpose of your particular book. That doesn't mean you have to throw those ideas away, but you can save them for another project or wait to see if there is a logical fit for them within your current project.

How do I clarify purpose?

In order to clarify the purpose of your writing, first think about your message. What is your topic? How did you choose that topic? Was it inspired by something you have been through or witnessed? Why is this important to you? Why would this be important to someone else?

When identifying the purpose of your writing, it will help to begin with the end in mind. I always ask my writers, "What are the five major goals you have for this book? What do you intend for this book to accomplish?"

Application

Here is an example of how to clarify your writing purpose:

I am writing a book about how to select an editor. My five goals are:

1) For the reader to learn about the different kinds of editing and be able to determine what level of service they need.
2) For the reader to understand the importance and necessity of editing.
3) To educate the reader about the value of an editor's time according to industry standards.
4) To teach the reader how to better prepare their manuscript to help them save

time and money during the editing process.
5) To guide the reader in choosing an editor that is best for them and their project.

To summarize my goals into the main purpose of this book, I would say: The purpose of my book about editing is to educate authors about the necessity of editing, help them understand the value and cost of editing and guide them in how to choose the editor that is best for them and their project.

Questions to Consider:

1. Why are you writing?
2. What is your topic?
3. How did you choose that topic?
4. Was it inspired by something you have been through or witnessed?
5. Why is this important to you?
6. Why would this be important to someone else?
7. What are the five major goals you have for this book?
8. What do you intend for this book to accomplish?"

CHAPTER TWO

Who am I Writing To?

Now that you know why you want to write and you know what you want your reader to receive from your writing, think about who you are writing to. Think about the fact that unless you plan to pour your heart out onto the page and then burn it or lock it away forever, there are real, living, breathing people that will one day behold the glorious words that you have penned. Technically your book is a one-way communication from you to your reader, although it is very possible that you will engage in conversation with your readers via book readings, online forums, etc. However, for the sake of creating something that will speak to the heart of your reader, let's imagine that your written communication is an intimate conversation between you and your reader. Are you telling them a story? Are you sharing information with them that you believe is life-changing or lifesaving?

What person or what group of people are looking for the information that you are presenting? Who is entertained by the type of story you are telling? Who benefits the most from what you are writing? Sometimes you may have a main audience in mind but there are other groups who will definitely benefit from your message as well. You may choose to focus on your primary target audience or you may want your writing to be inclusive and sensitive to other readers as well.

Your "why" should help you determine your "who." For example, it is easy to determine who I am writing a book about editing for: other writers. We often write for groups and communities that we belong to because that is our immediate sphere of influence and area of expertise. It is easy to write to someone when you know their heartbeat and you can readily identify with their situation, ideals, struggles, motivation, etc. This does not mean that you cannot write something to a group that you do not readily identify with. Since we are writing for other human beings, we can always find common ground if we really look for it.

When you define your target audience, you want to be as specific as possible. Think about who will benefit from your message the most. For example, if you are writing a book about parenting, is it for mothers and fathers? Are you writing about special parenting concerns? Are you writing to benefit parents of newborns, toddlers, children, pre-teens, teens, young adults, or special-needs children?

Depending on your topic and subject matter, you may want to also define the age group that you are targeting. I was editing a novel for a client whose target audience was single women aged 21-35. I questioned her reference to an actor that was considered extremely attractive by all women in the 1980s, because many women who fall into her target audience were children during that time. While some women would immediately understand the reference, for a large segment of the intended audience it could have created a distraction and made the story seem dated. In this instance, the definition of the target audience also aided in focusing the details of the story.

What is it that they need?

As you plan and as you write, you want to mentally check in with your intended audience. What is it that they need? In life, if we only gave people what we felt like giving them instead of considering their needs, likes, and dislikes, we could be considered selfish or unthoughtful. Even if you are presenting material that is challenging to your reader, you ultimately want to deliver something of value to them. You want them to consider their investments of time and/or money with your product to be well-spent.

Best-selling author, speaker, educator, television personality, and entrepreneur **Hasani Pettiford** (www.Hasani.com) says that when you write, you should ask yourself, "Who cares?" If you determine that your targeted reader really wouldn't care about or be impacted by some of the material you want to present, you may not want to include it. You should also ask yourself, "What does my reader care about?" when it comes to the subject matter that you are covering.

You should examine every goal and intention that you have for your project and ask yourself if your intended reader cares about that or why should they care about that. For example, in my work with writers I have been shocked to find out that editing is not always a top priority on their list of things to obtain for their project. This is something that people in my target audience may not care about but they should care about it. This means I may have to work a little harder to keep their interest by tapping into what they do care about.

In keeping with the editing book example, some writers may not see the necessity of paying an editor to review their manuscript because they believe they can proofread it themselves. I need to educate them about why it is important for them to invest in editing, even if they are the best proofreader in the world. They are not necessarily looking for this information, so why should they care?

One reason they will care about the information I have to offer is because I can demonstrate that I am an experienced author and editor and I know what I am talking about. I have done the research and I can present cases that support why it is important to hire the right editor for your project.

Writers will also care about my material because they want to look good. They don't want to publish a book that is full of errors and inconsistencies. They don't want all their hard work of writing to be poorly presented and thus, poorly received. It is near impossible for a person to edit themselves because our brain is able to fill in the blanks of what we intended to write.

It is my job to help my reader understand that according to the goals I outlined for my project.

It is your job to know what your reader cares about so you can deliver what is of value to them, even if they don't know it is of value to them yet. Confusing right? You may be thinking, "I am not a mind-reader, how am I supposed to know that?" You will be surprised by what you know when you take the time to really consider what is important. In the application section of this chapter, I will show you step-by-step how to tap into what your readers value, need, and want.

Why would they want to read my book?

If you don't take the extra steps to understand your target audience, your message with all its great intentions could fall flat. However, let us focus on the positive. In the beginning of this book, I mentioned how some of life's most memorable moments include the long-awaited, much–anticipated answers to our burning questions. You have the opportunity to be a monumental part of your readers' lives by providing the answers they have always wanted. In your consideration of your target audience, who they are and what is important to them, think about the questions they have and the answers you have for them.

How do I determine what questions my readers have?

There are several easy ways you can find out what questions your readers have and how you can answer them.

1) **Direct Interaction**: Have conversations with people who are in your target audience and find out directly from them what they are interested in. You can even create your own small focus groups with people who are your potential readers. Explain what you are working on and that you would like their help because you want to ensure that your content is

what people want and need. Folks appreciate when their opinion is valued and considered. You can reward them for their participation by giving them an advance copy of what you have created when it is finished.

2) **Internet Sleuthing**: With the abundance of social media outlets and online forums, you can do an internet search for communities that are made up of your target audience and people who are interested or potentially interested in your subject matter. Be a fly on the wall and observe the questions that people post in those forums and communities. It will also serve you to look at the answers that are posted in response to the questions. You can adjust your goals and intentions to meet the demand for information that you find. You can also discover how the information you offer and/or the delivery of that information differs from what is already out there.

3) **Surveys**: You can manually create a poll or survey, or use a service such as www.surveymonkey.com to create an attractive survey and post it via your social media pages or in your direct email campaigns as a quick and easy way to find out what your target audience wants and needs.
4) **Book Search**: If you are writing a book, you should conduct an online search of other books that cover the material you are writing about. This is not to turn you away from writing on the same topic, it is so you are aware of what knowledge is already being served so you can identify the opportunity to present your unique perspective. You can also apply what you have learned about your audience that perhaps is not being covered in the current body of work available in your field.

Back to the editing book example, I have been able to collect the questions of my clients and those who have made inquiries over the years. Because of my direct interaction with my target audience, as well as the research I do for my clients and my participation in different writing communities, I am confidently aware that when my reader or potential reader picks up my book, they want to know the following:

1) Why do I need an editor?
2) What can an editor do for me that I cannot do for myself?
3) What can I expect during an editing process?
4) How long does editing take? I have deadlines to meet.
5) How much does editing cost? Can I afford it?
6) How do I choose an editor?
7) Will the editor change my book? I don't want my message/voice/style to change.

Do you see how these potential reader questions fit in with the original goals I stated for my book?

1) For the reader to learn about the different kinds of editing and be able to determine what level of service they need.
2) For the reader to understand the importance and necessity of editing.
3) To educate the reader about the value of an editor's time according to industry standards.
4) To teach the reader how to better prepare their manuscript to help them save time and money in editing costs.
5) To guide the reader in choosing an editor that is best for them and their project.

When you use your goals along with the goals/questions of your reader, you will create something that serves their purpose and fulfills your desire to support, educate, or entertain your community. Use the interests and concerns of your reader to keep your writing honest and valuable for them. Filling pages with material that the readers don't need and are not interested in just proves your ability to fill pages with words. This is an opportunity to show your reader that not only can you offer something valuable to them, but that you care enough about them to provide something they can really use or enjoy.

Application

When I coached recording artist Marcel Anderson in the writing of his book, *Still Living, A Victimized Man's Journey*, we had several conversations about who he was writing for. Marcel knew he wanted to tell the story about how he as a man, dealt with being violently attacked and sexually assaulted but he was also interested in knowing who would want to read this book. Would his title appeal only to men and turn women away? Would men even want to read it due to the sensitive nature of the topic? We conducted internet searches using keywords like men and assault, men and domestic violence, men and abuse. Depending on what we searched for, we found information that focused on men as the abusers or men as the victims. We also found that there were not many books from the perspective of victimized men available, especially not when it came to personal accounts of abuse or assault. We found organizations that were set up to support men who have been victims of abuse, so we knew that Marcel had a potential audience who needed the support that he wanted to offer, even beyond those whom Marcel has had conversations with since he began publicly sharing the story of what happened to him.

From our informal poll of several women, we found that women were also interested in what Marcel had to say on the topic of abuse because of his unique perspective as a man, and because abuse is something that many women have dealt with as well. Marcel gleaned from his own experience as well as the fears, issues, and concerns that others shared with him to know what areas he needed to cover in his book. He knew that victims of abuse wanted and needed to know several things:

1) That they are not alone.

2) That no matter what the situation was, life is not over and there is a purpose for their life that they still have an opportunity to fulfill.
3) That even though it can be difficult to do, it is necessary to speak up about what happened to you if you have been abused.
4) That what others may have said or done to abuse you does not define who you are.
5) The necessity of forgiveness and learning how to trust again.
6) The importance of having the support of others to help you heal from what you have experienced.
7) The role of faith in the process of healing, forgiveness, and discovering your life's purpose.

It is important to note that even with the wealth of knowledge that Marcel already had about his topic and his audience, he continued to poll others for their feedback. As he completed major portions of his book he shared it with a select group of people in order to make sure that the messages he intended to deliver were communicated clearly and to discover where he could add more clarity.

Questions to Consider:

1. Are you telling a story?
2. Are you sharing information that you believe is life-changing or lifesaving?
3. What person or what group of people are looking for the information that you are presenting?
4. Who is entertained by the type of story you are telling?
5. Who benefits the most from what you are writing?
6. What makes your message or story unique?
7. What questions do you think your readers have on this topic?
8. What questions have people already asked on this topic?
9. What information do you have to add to the answers that already exist?
10. What unique perspective can you bring to the questions and answers that already exist?

CHAPTER THREE

How do I Keep Track of all This?

If you have been considering all of the questions that I have asked you within the first two chapters, you should have a lot of notes by now. If you have really been digging then you should also have quite a bit of research. How do you keep track of all that, especially if you are acquiring information while you are 'on-the-go' or just happen to pick up some brilliant inspiration in the midst of conversation with your associates?

I personally arm myself with a few different ways to capture my notes, inspiration, and musings. While I am still in the brainstorming phase of my process and not really thinking about sitting down to write yet, I use an app in my phone for a program called **Evernote**. I like Evernote because I can quickly capture ideas right in my phone which is almost always handy and I can easily share those notes via email so that I can copy and paste or do whatever else I need to do. In case technology fails me or just isn't convenient at the moment, I also always have a small notebook stashed in my purse.

Once I get ready to write, I will take those notes which include my big ideas for the project and my goals and begin to construct an outline. Generally, the goals and big ideas will be chapter headings and I list them in the order that I think I want them to appear in the book. For each chapter heading, I will identify at least three major points that should be covered within that chapter and add those to the outline. These major points should be fueled by your target audience research as well as support the goals you have for each chapter.

As an example, here is part of an early version of the outline for this book:

I. Define Purpose
II. Define Audience
   a. Who are you writing to?
   b. What is it that they need?
   c. Why would they want to read your book?
III. Define Message
   a. What is it you want them to know?
   b. Where is the material for your message?
IV. Make it Real
   a. Authenticity
   b. Brokenness
   c. Compassion

Please notice that I said this is part of an earlier version of this book's outline. Your outline is a tool and a guide for you to use, not a rigid, set-in-stone, permanent list for your book. You can change it and tweak it as much as you want throughout your writing process, as it is not unusual for a writer to change direction or find more material that they would like to include.

Some people find it useful to map out or diagram their ideas before using an outline or instead of using an outline. I learned this technique many years ago in school and we called it a sunburst or clustering.

Example of a Sunburst

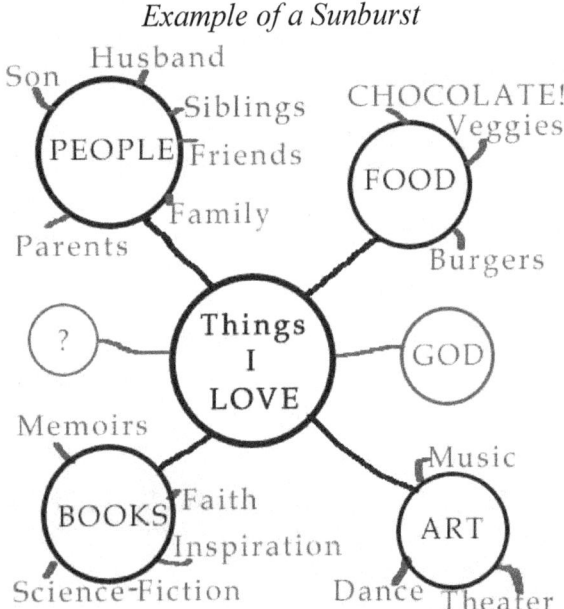

If you were to construct an outline for your book using the sunburst on the previous page, it would look something like this:

Things I Love

I. Introduction
II. GOD
III. People
    a. Husband
    b. Son
    c. Parents
    d. Siblings
    e. Family
    f. Friends
IV. Food
    a. Chocolate
    b. Veggies
    c. Burgers
V. Art
    a. Music
    b. Theater
    c. Dance
VI. Conclusion

Application

Of course those are very simple and basic examples, but I believe it is better that way for our purposes. Sunbursts work great freehand with a piece of scrap paper and a pencil. If you want to simplify further, you can list all your thoughts, questions, and ideas on one sheet of paper, then on another sheet of paper begin to cluster them and form the sunburst. From there you can create your outline which will be the structure for your book. You can tweak it as often and as many times as you like, as long as you are not driving yourself crazy.

Fill in your sunburst and your outline with everything you want your readers to know after reading your book and everything you think they would want to know after reading your book.

Questions to Consider

1. How will I capture and save my thoughts and ideas?
2. What method of organization works best for me?

Chapter Four

What Do I Want them to Know?

For the remainder of this book, I want to refrain from using examples from other projects because I want you to think only of your own project. You can always refer back to the examples to help you stay on track. This is the fun and sometimes most difficult part – the work of actually digging deep and providing substance for your reader.

Once you are clear on your topic and have at least a basic framework for where your project is going you can begin writing or clarify what you have already written. I do not believe that you need to have a whole structure in place before you begin writing, but I do believe it is necessary to have a structure in place in order to complete your project and write it with excellence.

That may be confusing, so I will elaborate. Sometimes the pressure of trying to figure out exactly what you are doing and trying to map it all out can hamper your creativity. You may be trying to fit your thoughts into the box of the book you think you are going to write, which prevents your thoughts and ideas from flowing freely. Therefore, I think it is helpful to have a period or season of free writing until your true message emerges. There is no structure for that, you just write whatever is on your heart and mind to write until you feel that you are "on to something," or "the light bulb turns on" or you have a major epiphany that, "A Hah! This is what I want to write my book about!"

Do not feel constricted in any way by how the writing process is "supposed to look." You could have a dream one night and be able to map out your entire project based on that dream. You may have been engaging in conversations for several years that have finally culminated into a book that you are about to birth. You may have a loose structure and be able to write a couple of chapters in one sitting but may find it to be a slower process for other chapters. You may get halfway through the project and decide to switch gears. Do not despair, this just means that you are really writing! When you feel stuck or as if you are getting off track, go back and reflect on your goals.

Where is the material coming from?

As you write, always consider what it is that you want your readers to know, what questions they have based on your research, and how you will answer their questions. If you are writing a memoir, what parts of your life will you write about? How much are you willing to tell? What details and events will raise further questions for your readers? If you are writing with the intention to inform your readers on a certain subject, you must have an abundance of information on your topic in order to accomplish your goals and fill in any blanks that your readers may have. This is not to say that you must write all the information there ever is to know on your particular topic. However, you do want to create a work of substance that provokes the response you are looking for and sets you apart from other writers on that topic.

Application

You cannot fill the pages of a book with anything worthwhile unless you are well-informed on your subject. Even with works of fiction, your story cannot be "real" unless you are able to fill in the details to make it real. You as the writer must become a student of the world and the lives you are creating for your characters.

Now that you know what you want to write about and you are in touch with what your readers want and need, conduct additional research. Get to know who are the reliable sources or experts in your field. Learn from them, study new techniques, read as much as you can, and pay attention to current events and the world around you.

Questions to Consider

1. What is it you want your readers to know?
2. How will you answer the questions they have?
3. Where is the material that you are drawing from? Is it credible and reliable?
4. If you are writing about your life, how much are you willing to share?
    a. Are you sharing enough to answer your readers' questions adequately?
    b. Are you painting a vivid image for the reader to be able to experience your life as you tell it?
5. Are you using technical words or phrases that all your readers may not understand? Do you need to define and explain these words?
6. Are there gaps in your story that could be confusing or distracting to your readers?

Chapter Five

Is it Real Yet?

My challenge to you as you write is to find the love in what you are trying to accomplish. What do you love so much that could inspire you, motivate you, and drive you to complete this project? If love was the motivating factor behind your writing, think about how powerful that would be:

1. LOVE connects you with your passion- it adds energy and excitement to what you are doing.
2. LOVE will cause you to be real, authentic, transparent, and honest even if it doesn't feel good because you know it will benefit the people or cause that you love.

3. LOVE will cause you to seek out the truth and research the important information that your readers need to know on a particular subject.
4. LOVE will push you to completion because you know that someone needs to read your message, your story, or your life-saving information.
5. LOVE will supply the "why" when you are frustrated and start wondering why you are even putting yourself through the process.
6. LOVE will drive you to complete every element of your project in excellence because you wouldn't present someone you love with anything less than your best.

What is the LOVE factor behind your writing? Is it the love of God, your children, your spouse, your family, the community you are trying to help, the readers of the world, or the professionals of your industry? Is it the love of being able to create something that brings income and other resources? What you love is personal and effective in being a driving force behind your writing.

Authenticity

Merriam-Webster defines authenticity as, "real or genuine: not copied or false; true and accurate." Allow this to be an internal check as you write, especially since you are being motivated by love. Is the information you are presenting true or fabricated? Are you simply making statements because they sound good and may get a rise out of some people or are you writing something that could have a profound, lasting effect? Are your statements based on fact or speculation? Anyone can write about something they overheard or a rumor that has been circulating. That doesn't require any extra thought or work. However, love causes you to be diligent in making sure that what you present is honest.

It may seem that these statements would only apply to works of nonfiction, however, how many times have you read something or watched a program that was completely unoriginal, tired, and 'played out?' You feel cheated when you give your time and energy to something when it becomes obvious that the creator didn't think enough of their audience to truly create something new rather than present a cheap copy. It could be tempting to use popular scenarios, phrases, and clichés but what will your reader be left with when they put your book down if that is all you offered?

Brokenness

I like the word 'brokenness' because it sounds like a really super-deep or spiritual way of saying humility. When you want someone to understand a particular message because you realize how important it has been to your own life that you received that message, you are getting in touch with your own brokenness. This is not a place of, "I have it all together and I know what I am talking about so you need to pay attention to whatever I'm writing." This is a place of, "I love you. I care about those who have dealt with this particular issue. I understand how it feels; I have been there. I want to share with you how I dealt with that because I know how frustrating/confusing/painful/etc. that can be. I want to help you."

Take a moment and think about how you can apply this principle of brokenness to your project. What connects you with your readers? What have you felt that is probably similar to what they are feeling? What information do you have that can help them?

Compassion

Brokenness and compassion go hand in hand. It is hard to be judgmental of someone when you are in touch with the fact that you were once in the very same predicament they are now in. You were once facing the same challenges that they now face. You were once just as clueless and had the same millions of questions that they have. Be honest with your readers, give them the information they need, but be compassionate while doing so. Understand that the truth often hurts, especially when someone may not be ready to fully accept it. They may not want to admit that the way they have been doing things is wrong; they may not want to learn new skills; they may not want the real answer. Part of them may not want the truth, but part of them does, and that is why they are reading your book.

Application

As you write, keep a mental check on yourself to always be genuine and honest, original, humble and compassionate.

Questions to Consider

1. What is the love behind your purpose for writing?
2. With every sentence, are you being authentic?
3. If you are using research or statements made by someone else, have you given them credit within your project?
4. Have you brought your own creativity and originality to the subject?
5. Are you empathizing with your readers and writing from a place of humility and a real desire to help?

Chapter Six

Did I Wrap it in Love?

In the last chapter I shared the importance of finding the love behind what you are writing. When love is involved, you generally give the best that you have to give. You are thoughtful, considerate, and purposeful in your actions. Your writing and the presentation of your writing should be the same way. If the contents of your book are written in love, then shouldn't they also be wrapped in love? Your book is an expression of love, so it must be presented with excellence.

If you have followed my advice so far in organizing and outlining your thoughts, researching your audience and subject, following your outline as you write, and keeping your audience and goals in mind the entire time, then you have already been operating in excellence to write your book. Your work does not end there, however, you must ensure that the finished product is delivered into your readers' hands with the highest level of clarity, readability, professionalism, and attractiveness that you can offer.

Editing

Every writer needs a good editor if they desire to share their writing with the world. You know what you intend to write, so that is quite possibly what you see when you look at your written text. A good editor will identify whether you have clearly communicated your message and ensure your text is grammatically correct and free of typos. When you consider the cost of publishing your book, the major portion of your budget should be for editing alone. Ideally you want an editor who is experienced with your genre and type of writing. Find out how the editing process works. Will the editor perform one round of editing and simply tell you what to fix, or will they collaborate with you and provide several rounds of editing if necessary? Will they proofread only for typos or will they review your content to ensure clarity and consistency?

(You can review standard industry rates for editorial services here:
[Editorial Freelancers Association](#))

Graphic Design and Formatting:

Your potential consumers will most definitely judge your book by its cover so you want to reserve another good portion of your budget for a designer who is experienced in creating attractive book covers. Book cover design is not the same as creating other marketing materials, there are certain elements that must be included on a book cover in order for it to meet industry standards. You also want to a book cover that can hold its own on a shelf with other books. What will attract someone to your book over the next book on the shelf?

You should also make sure that the interior of your book is formatted not just for printer specifications, but well-organized and pleasing to the eye. You can hire someone to do this, or, you can use a book template and tweak it to your liking.

Application

Think about all the work that went into the writing of your book and commit to presenting your hard work to the public in the best possible way. Begin to research editors and graphic designers that you will feel comfortable working with who will give you great value for your money while providing the service that you absolutely need. Do not compromise when it comes to presenting your work with excellence.

Questions to Consider

1. Have you wrapped your project in love by hiring a team to edit, format, and design great graphics for it?
2. If you will do your own formatting or graphics, are you familiar with publishing industry standards and requirements?
3. In your search for an editor/formatter/graphic designer, what is their experience with book publishing? Can you read testimonials from their customers? Can you see samples of their work? Have they answered all of your questions satisfactorily?
4. Should you decide to work with a publishing company to produce and distribute your book, what services are included in their pricing? Do the packages include services that you absolutely need? Are there any hidden costs? Does the company produce titles that you would want your book to be listed among? What other services does the company offer that you could potentially need?

Conclusion

Leaving it All on the Page

There is a lot of work involved in writing a book that truly makes an impact on its readers but when love is involved, passion takes over and fuels you for the journey. When you take the time to write with your readers in mind, you create a bond with your audience that is not easily broken or forgotten. Imagine, you can provide the answer that your readers have been seeking all along!

Anything is Possible

Years ago, I read a book that opened many doors for me. I was repeatedly engaging in relationships that were just simply not what I needed and I didn't know how to stop. When I realized how badly this pattern was affecting my life, I actually prayed for help with a prayer that went something like, "God if you don't intervene, I already know I am just going to keep doing what I have always been doing. I need help." My prayer was answered when a friend introduced me to a book entitled, *The Plural Thing* by Linda Dominique Grosvenor-Holland.

This book contained all the answers I needed, at precisely the time that I was looking for them. I devoured the book in its entirety and began applying it to my life. I sought out the author and whatever other programs she had going on. To my delight, Mrs. Holland made herself available to anyone who had questions and was struggling in their relationships. No one could have predicted what would happen next.

As I applied Mrs. Holland's writings and teachings to my life, I stopped putting so much energy into chasing relationships and instead focused on my relationship with God and myself. I began writing again. I found out that Mrs. Holland also taught courses on book publishing and I took her course. A year or so later, I married my best friend and Dominique (as we now call her) and her husband Calvin participated in our wedding ceremony. Two years after that, I published my first book and one year after that, my editing and coaching business grew into a publishing company.

Several great people have contributed to success in my personal life and my career and I have mentioned them within this work, however, the clear turning point for me was when I read Linda Dominique Grosvenor-Holland's hard-hitting, authentic, loving, generously thorough book about how to "spiritually prepare for your soul-mate." Dominique, who is my mentor and friend to this day, did not even know what would happen when a once-confused girl read her book and allowed it to penetrate her life.

You have the potential to write something that will spark major change in someone's life by your willingness to get in tune with your audience and share the truth with excellence, generosity and love.

What's Your Story?

Interview with Author Marcel Anderson

Marcel Anderson is a national recording artist and bestselling author who hired Rain Publishing to guide him through his writing process as well as edit and publish his first book, *Still Living: A Victimized Man's Journey*.

Many of the questions featured in this book were used during the coaching process to help Marcel tell his deeply personal and sensitive story about being held at gunpoint, brutally attacked and sexually assaulted and his process of healing from that situation. Here is what Marcel had to say about the coaching and publishing process:

How did Rain Publishing help you in the writing of your book?

MA - Rain Publishing was very helpful during my writing process. I don't think this book would have turned out the way it did without their support. Rain Publishing's process helped motivate, inspire and cultivate the writer inside me. They constantly encouraged me to search deeper within my own story. The questions Rain Publishing asked during the writing phase pushed me to write the truth in a meaningful way. The questions really guided my thought process.

What challenges did you have to overcome while writing your book?

MA - During my writing process I overcame so many challenges, including the challenge of writing my book within a certain timeframe. I also overcame the fear of telling my personal sexual assault story, something that many men don't do on a regular basis. I grew more confident because they strongly supported me throughout this process.

What services did you receive from Rain Publishing?

During my writing process, Rain Publishing provided editing support and mentored me through the journey of writing my personal story. They went over and beyond the call of duty in order for my book to get published. They met the expectations of God and myself. We were all on one accord and I truly believe that is important when it comes to collaboration and teamwork. It takes a team in order to accomplish the intended goal and I believe that was completed because Rain Publishing did their part.

Did the team understand your vision? If so, how was that displayed throughout the process?

MA - I truly received personal service throughout this writing process. We constantly met in person and over the phone to map out the vision I had for my book. I knew what I wanted it to be and felt like Rain Publishing supported me throughout the entire writing journey. I truly believe they understood my vision. After long talks about what I thought the presentation of my book should look like, it all came together and the task was completed.

To learn more about Marcel Anderson, visit www.MarcelAnderson.com

ABOUT THE AUTHOR

Speaker, author, editor, and writing coach Rachel Renee Smith is committed to empowering people to obtain spiritual and emotional healing that frees them to enjoy their lives and have fruitful relationships. She communicates with love and transparency through her writing and speaking to demonstrate that acceptance, divine provision, purpose, and real love are available to all through God. With a B.S. degree in communication from Seton Hall University and an M.B.A. from the University of Phoenix, Rachel uses her knowledge and expertise to mentor, coach, and assist students, writers, and entrepreneurs through her company, Rain Publishing. She has also authored two devotionals entitled, The Rain Won't Hide These Tears and While the Sun Still Shines and is the co-founder of the Women's Life Support Group and Lavender Rain Beauty, Books, and Gifts, both based in North Carolina. She has a bright and talented son and is married to her best friend and partner in ministry, Jeffrey LaMont Smith, who is a speaker, life skills educator, and co-founder of Rain Publishing.

Connect with Rachel:
www.RachelReneeSmith.com
www.Facebook.com/rachelreneesmith
www.Twitter.com/RachelRenee_S

Rain Publishing provides writing, editing, and self-publishing services for authors and entrepreneurs who have messages that inspire, encourage, uplift, educate, and build faith in God.

We partner with you to ensure that your voice, style, and message are captured and conveyed the way you want them to be.

Whether you have finished writing your manuscript or haven't started writing yet, we can help!

Our Services

- Writing Coach Services
- Book Publishing Services
- Editing Services
- Design Services
- Marketing Assistance
- Memoir Writing

Testimonials

"There are times when God calls on you to do a certain thing and you do not have the skills necessary to complete the task. This is exactly where I found myself when I felt led by God to write books on marriage and relationships. I knew how to put my thoughts on paper, however, editing, publishing, formatting and all of the technical aspects of publishing were beyond my knowledge. In my pursuit for a publisher, Rain Publishing came highly recommended. Although cautious in my approach, my first conversation with Rachel Renee Smith placed me at ease. I immediately sensed that this business was more than a business, it is a ministry. She fully understood what I was trying to accomplish and took control of this project as if it were her own..."

-Winston Tyrone Jackson, Sr., Author of Marriage, 21 Years of Doing it Wrong, 21 Days to Make it Right, and Preparing to Date Your Soul Mate
www.winstontyronejacksonsr.com

"Rain Publishing is a reputable publishing company that produces a quality product that both you and your readers can be proud of. Their knowledge base, professionalism, timely process, and attention to every detail are the reasons I choose Rain Publishing every time."

—Hasani Pettiford, Award-Winning Author, Speaker, TV Personality, and Founder of Couples Academy www.Hasani.com, www.CouplesAcademy.org

"When it was time to re-edit my book, The Plural Thing: Spiritually Preparing for Your Soul Mate, I trusted my voice with Rachel. I'm so thrilled I did. I was not disappointed. I found her services to be superior to any I've used before…"

Linda Dominique Grosvenor Holland, Author, Coach, Founder of Love Better Institute www.LindaDominiqueGrosvenor.com

"As an aspiring author, Rain Publishing has helped fulfill my dream plus more! They are very proficient and their knowledge is valuable. The finished product Rain Publishing helped me create has become a success!"

—*Ronda Lynette Henry, Speaker and Author of The Caged Bird Does Sing*
http://rondalynnettehenry.com/

"I am a first time author. The only thing I knew for sure was that I had to give birth to my book. God sent me a midwife in the form of Rachel Renee Smith. Rachel helped me organize my thoughts and write my story from the heart. She coached and guided me through the completion of my manuscript. I don't believe in mistakes. God ordained our paths to cross. He knew that Rain Publishing had just what I needed. I can't wait to work with her on my second book."

—*Annette Johnson, The FLY Coach*
http://www.theflycoach.com/

"Rachel is a genius when it comes to editing. I have experienced her work with two of my books. Her diligence is what makes her stand out above the rest. She makes sure that she does what she says when it comes to time and additional reviews. I would definitely recommend Rachel without question because it is hard to find an editor who is as thorough as her. When your final review comes back there are never any mishaps. She is the epitome of business and efficiency."

Candra Ward, Speaker, Trainer, Author, Entrepreneur, Licensed Educational Instructor, and Mentor www.CandraWard.com

Thank you for purchasing this book! If this book has helped you, please leave a review on your favorite online retailer's website.

To order more titles by Rachel Renee Smith, Please visit www.RainPublishing.com

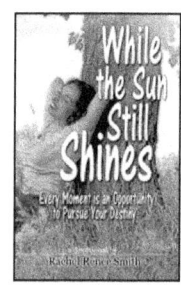

www.ingramcontent.com/pod-product-compliance
Lightning Source LLC
Chambersburg PA
CBHW072104290426
44110CB00014B/1825